CLASSIC
INSULTS

Intelligent Abuse To Keep The Idiots At Bay

BB

Our greatest danger could be your stupidity.

Fortune Cookie

He has all the virtues I dislike and none of the vices I admire.

Sir Winston Churchill

You, my friend, are a barmpot and a loon.

A sharp tongue
is no indication
of a sharp mind.

He has no enemies,
but is intensely disliked
by his friends.

Oscar Wilde

The problem is that you lack the power of conversation, but not the power of speech.

I'd love to ask how old you are, but unfortunately I know you can't count that high.

Why do you sit there looking like an envelope without any address on it?

Mark Twain

If the words I say offend you, imagine the ones I keep to myself.

Somewhere in Fairy Tale Land, a bridge is missing its troll.

There is nothing wrong with you that reincarnation won't cure.

Jack E. Leonard

The reason I'm smiling
is because I can't hear
a word you're saying.

Are you always this silly or are you just making a special effort today?

He can compress the most words into the smallest idea of any man I know.

Abraham Lincoln

Somebody's boring me.
I think it's you.

Dylan Thomas

You only have one annoying habit. Breathing.

You, minion,
are too saucy.

Shakespeare: Two Gentlemen of Verona

I'll never forget the first time I met you, no matter how hard I try.

If you were on fire and
I had a glass of water,
I'd drink it.

No more sense of direction than a bunch of firecrackers.

Rob Wagner

I’m not insulted by your opinion, because I see no value in it.

No, no. I’m yawning because I’m *interested.*

He knows nothing
and thinks he knows
everything.

George Bernard Shaw

I won't waste my breath on an insult. It'll never be as good as the one nature gave you.

He is not only dull himself; he is the cause of dullness in others.

Samuel Johnson

Whatever angle we look at this from, the result is the same: you're full of crap.

I used to think you were
a pain in the neck, but now
I have a lower opinion.

I do desire we may be better strangers.

Shakespeare: As You Like It

I have tried seeing things
from your point of view,
but I can't get my head
that far up my backside.

Don't think out loud. You're lowering our collective IQ.

But oh... to sit next to a man who has spent his whole life in trying to educate others! What a dreadful experience that is!

Oscar Wilde

A year from now, I'll still be wishing you were somewhere else.

Sorry, I don't have time to ignore you right now.

I have nothing but respect for you – and not much of that.

Groucho Marx

Why don't you take a nice relaxing trip... off the end of the earth?!

You may not have lost
all of your marbles,
but there's definitely
a hole in the bag.

It isn't that I'm not a people person, I'm just not a *stupid* people person.

I’ve had a perfectly wonderful evening, but this wasn’t it.

Groucho Marx

Carry on rolling your eyes, you might find your brain back there.

Do you need some toilet paper for all that crap you're talking?

He has delusions of adequacy.

Walter Kerr

What doesn't kill you...
disappoints me.

He never chooses an opinion; he just wears whatever happens to be in style.

Leo Tolstoy

You think I'm funny?
That's because you're not
clever enough to understand
I'm being horrible.

He loves nature in spite of what it did to him.

Forrest Tucker